these moonlit musings belong to:

_____

Notes for the Night

RP Studio™
Hachette Book Group
1290 Avenue of the Americas, New York, NY 10104
www.runningpress.com
@Running_Press

Printed in China

First Edition: August 2022

Published by RP Studio, an imprint of Perseus Books, LLC, a
subsidiary of Hachette Book Group, Inc. The RP Studio name and
logo are trademarks of the Hachette Book Group.

The publisher is not responsible for websites (or their content) that
are not owned by the publisher.

Design by Susan Van Horn

ISBN: 978-0-7624-7430-1

1010

10 9 8 7 6 5 4 3 2 1

Notes for the Night

A GUIDED JOURNAL FOR MOONLIT MAGIC

MAIA TOLL

illustrated by
LUCILLE CLERC

RP **STUDIO**

PHILADELPHIA

WELCOME TO THE INTERSTITIAL SPACES OF THE NIGHT.

Without the glow of electric lights, the evening hours become what they've always been: a breath of mystery, a place where reality tastes different on your tongue. As daylight fades, you'll come to know the many shades of gray that make up both the universe and your own psyche.

The Night is not a place of absolutes. As you jot your thoughts and explorations down in this journal, dare to question your daytime truths and what you think you know or believe. Ask yourself to avoid the linear. Think instead in circles and spirals and shooting stars. Every question you ponder will lead you closer not to *the* truth but to *your* truth.

None of the exercises in this journal need to make sense by the light of day. The logic of light has nothing to do with the dream spaces of Night's darkness. Don't think too hard. Simply follow the strands of intuition and inner knowing.

By diving into the unknown and writing it down, you'll find not only yourself, but also the lost magic of the world—the place where serendipity lives and you can only see the truth out of the corner of your eye.

magic is everywhere.

TO SEE IT AND THE EFFECTS
IT HAS ON YOUR LIFE, change
the way you perceive the world.

TO HARNESS IT, change the
way you interact with the
energies around you.

TO KNOW IT, change the way
you think.

TO LIVE IT, remember the
lessons of the Night as you go
about your day.

Think of this mantra as your starting point. If you're ever stuck on a certain prompt, return to this precept. Meditate on the words and allow them to open you back up to the mystic.

How does this mantra make you feel? What does it mean to you? Feel free to create your own Night mantra.

When the final pinks of day have faded into dusk's dove gray, come to the page to ponder and soak in the wonders of the Night. Focus first on your sense of sight. When the light of the sun is removed, what remains? Are the trees in your yard limned in silver? Is your garden made of moonbeams? Observe the Night's landscape without judgment, noticing what you see and what you don't. How do familiar things look once shrouded in darkness?

What does the Night sound like? Focus less on cars driving by or your neighbor's dog barking and more on what exists in the sliver of starlight in between . . . Try opening your eyes and closing them. Does this change what you hear? If the Night were a song, what song would it be? Do you hear creatures? Are they on the ground? In the sky? In a tree? Can you tell just based on what you hear, or is sound itself fluid and strange in the blackness of Night?

How does the Night feel on your skin? Is it a blanket or a butterfly kiss? Is the Night air humid, playful, sensuous, chilly?

What do you smell standing under the Night sky?
(Is it strange to be sniffing the Night? How does it feel
for you?)

Open your mouth and taste the night. Yes, it will feel . . . unusual. Do it anyway. Let the Night wrap around your tongue so you can savor the notes of menthol and mystery. Record what you experience, and see what it sparks within you.

Open yourself fully to the Night, allowing all your senses to sing simultaneously, and return to the cosmic question: Who are you in the Night? Gently notice how your Nighttime knowings differ from the knowings of your daytime self.

Ask what the Night has to share with you. Pay careful, but soft, attention to its reply. Practice observing and noticing. Remember, you're not deciding whether these noticings are good or bad; you're just letting them land like snowflakes on your winter mittens.

Gather observations from time spent outdoors so you can write a Night Haiku. A haiku is a type of short-form nature poem, three lines long, which originated in 13th-century Japan. The lines needn't rhyme, but you do have to count the syllables:

* Five for the first line

* Seven for the second

* Five for the third

If you aren't satisfied with your first haiku, write another. Poem-writing is a practice you can return to Night after Night (as is the case with most of the exercises in this journal). Let each haiku take you deeper into noticing the Night around you.

Into the falling
needles of night, perfect stars
poke holes in the dark.

Hush, green frog burping
in the miasma. Owl will
ruin your dreaming.

Mercury rose fast,
a flaming needle, streaking
through velvet sky dreams.

In our modern world, we use electric lights to ease the duality between day and Night. Most of us have forgotten the flavor of true darkness.

Choose a Night to go dark. Turn off all electronics, and don't use flashlights or electric lamps. If you have streetlights near your windows, draw the curtains. Use candlelight or battery-operated tea lights to keep the light soft.

Do your thoughts change when you're in true dark? Do the things you're willing to discuss with your partner or family shift? Does your writing flow in a different way? Do you desire different books or drinks or ways of sitting? In the dark, can you relinquish your daylight persona and rewrite the rules of being yourself?

Before we go further, pause and think about why are you interested in unraveling the mysteries of being human? Why is the mystic appealing to you? Will you begin to heal yourself? Guide others to heal? Create something new in the world? Explore the places where sciences and magic meet? Begin a sacred practice? Create sacred spaces for others? Be honest with yourself about what you are seeking.

Let's explore some magical precepts. First, everything starts with a spark of energy; everything holds the energy of its own beginning.

It's harder to find that spark of energy in mass-produced objects. But it's there. Can you think of some inanimate objects that feel alive to you? Look around you right at this moment. What feels alive to you? What doesn't? Why?

Choose something that feels plastic-y and inanimate. Now, in your imagination, trace its story all the way back to its beginnings. Imagine the process by which it was conceived and made. Allow your eyes to open to all the creative energy behind this object. How many people put a little bit of themselves into its creation? Can you find its spark?

Now try it with something alive: trace the story of the last vegetable you ate back to its beginning. Write about the farmer who sowed the seed of the plant that will grow until it eventually produces the very vegetable you ate.

What if science and myth are not a duality but instead two ways of expressing the same concepts? What would happen if you believed you could explore an idea either through scientific thinking or magical thinking and get the same result? *Science is simply daytime's version of Nighttime magic.*

When you curl up in your bed to go to sleep tonight, set your intention to consult your dreams and see if they concur. Tomorrow morning describe here what happened in your dream. What do you believe it was trying to tell you?

Alchemy is an ancient science that can support your soul work by helping you untangle thoughts and emotions that are keeping you stuck and stagnant. To begin the process, list some problems in your life that you are interested in working through.

Choose one of the problems from your list to undergo the alchemical process. The first step is to *Separate:* Put your problem, issue, or tangled thoughts in the middle of a Mind Map, then tease out the individual strands of challenging thoughts and emotions you want to unbind.

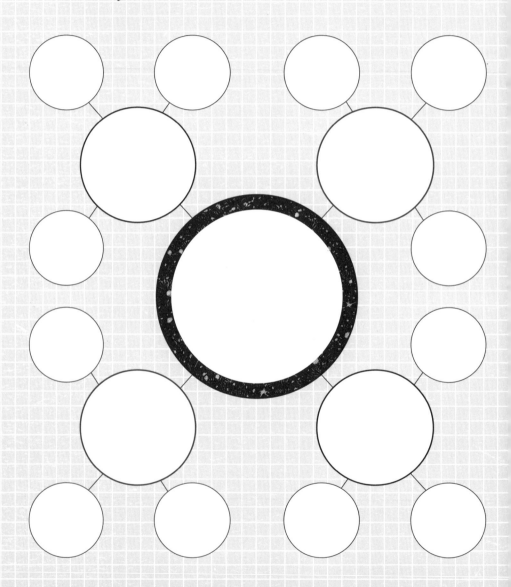

The next step is to *Purify:* Work with each individual strand of thought or emotion to clear it and find resolution within yourself.

Say your central concern is that you want to be a forest ranger, but your family is pushing you to become a brain surgeon. One strand of this larger issue is that you're angry at your mother for not seeing you as you see yourself.

Work on purifying one strand in the following pages by writing a letter to the person or people involved. Remember that the "people involved" might just be the many sides of your own personality! After you write the letter, burn it to symbolize that you're releasing the hold of that emotion on your choices, or releasing yourself from unrealistic expectations. Alternately, you can actually send the letter in order to open a door to further conversation between yourself and the recipient.

When sending mail, it's better to send a *letter* as opposed to an *email*. The surprise of receiving a piece of paper and a stamp will get you a more thoughtful response than an electronic message.

The final step in this alchemy is to *Bring It All Back Together:* Everything is interconnected. After you've unbraided the threads and purified each one, examine the patterns that emerged through the process. For instance, if you've realized in the above example that your mom does love you but just has a different idea about what's right for your life, you can stop taking her behavior personally, realizing it's her issue, not yours. Purification changes how you see things. So once you purify, reexamine the original issue. Now that your thoughts aren't tangled, you will probably clearly see the root of your problem and be able to work to resolve it. Maybe you initially thought you'd simply stop talking to your mom in order to feel free to do what you want with your life. Post-purification you might decide to have an honest conversation with her, knowing that Mom's love for you will win her over in the end.

Maybe you've heard that change is the only constant. Still can be overwhelming. Small changes can help make big changes feel easier. Try going to bed at a different time than you're used to, rearranging the furniture in your bedroom, upending the order of your bedtime routine, or putting new things on your nightstand.

Notice what this does to your senses. Do you feel more alert? Are you being more intentional about how you go about your evening and move within your space?

Try changing a habit that doesn't serve you, a negative attitude about something (or someone), or an old perspective that needs a good dust-off. When you purposely step into change, you start noticing the nuances of the world around you again. How does it feel, stepping into change? What nuances do you notice? Can you feel a new adventure that the change might be announcing?

*L*et's talk about energy. Energy follows intention. Wherever you intend your attention to go, your energy will follow.

When you set an intention, be super-clear about what you want. Put your intention in the center of this Mind Map and brainstorm all the things it touches. Let's say you intend to take a trip to see the Great Wall of China. If you have a family, this will affect them. Your job will also need to be considered. And, of course, if you have 11 cats counting on you for their dinner, they too will have to be taken into account.

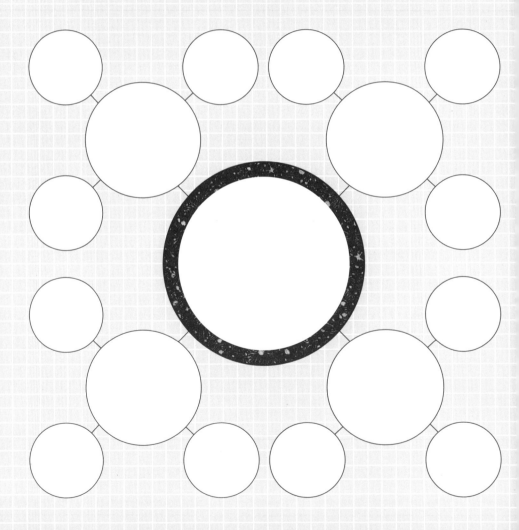

In fairy tales wishes often go awry. In the tale of the Monkey's Paw, an older couple is given a magical, wish-granting monkey's paw. They ask the paw for money to pay off their house. The money comes from a payout that is a result of their only son being killed in a work accident. In another, somewhat silly, tale from Sweden, a woman is granted three wishes and, knowing her husband will come home hungry, wishes for a sausage. Her husband arrives, and she tells him of the wishes and presents the sausage. The man grows enraged. "You silly woman!" he hollers. "You had three wishes and you wasted one on a sausage? I wish that sausage was stuck to your nose!" And the sausage sticks to her nose. The couple must use the last wish to remove the sausage.

These tales prompt us to be mindful of what we're intending. Remember an intention is merely a wish with some oomph behind it. So how can you be meticulously thoughtful with your intentions?

One thing that's often neglected in intention setting is checking for preexisting roadblocks that stand between you and your intention. What might these be?

* Your own negative self-talk
* Fear
* Jealousy
* Old thought patterns
* Lack of money or other resources

Write down everything you see as an obstacle and what you might do to remove these blocks.

Your intention needs to be fed. It's hungry for your attention and action. There's an old cartoon of a man praying. His prayer is "Please let me win the lottery, God!" God's reply is "Help me out: buy a ticket!"

Help your intention out. Once you set your clear intention, choose three action steps to help it manifest. Then do them.

Picture in your mind that something you are intending has already happened. This is called *visualization*. How would your day look, how would it be different, if your intention became a reality? Imagine as many details as possible in your visualization.

Balance is found in understanding opposites and, by understanding them, being able to shift away from the extremes and come to center. Take a moment to celebrate balance and notice all the places you experience (or don't experience!) equilibrium in your life.

Everything is connected to everything else, even if you can't figure out how. The early psychotherapist Carl Jung believed that this level of interconnectedness extended to human minds and spirits. He posited that each of us has a direct link to something he called the *collective unconscious*. The collective unconscious is like a giant dreams- cape that we all get to play in. It's the place from which all of our symbols, archetypes, and rituals originate. When you daydream or Night-dream, you're dipping into the collective unconscious. If an ancient labyrinth design in Thailand looks surprisingly similar to one in New Mexico, which also bears a distinct resemblance to one from Crete, or a ceremony from Egypt is strikingly similar to one performed in Iceland, it's because all of these cultures dipped into the same collective unconscious.

The most important practice for figuring out interconnections is observation. Much of what goes on in the world around us fails to catch our notice, and so much of what we dream is lost when we wake.

Choose a color and decide to see at least 10 things in that hue over the course of the Night. Do you notice things you hadn't paid attention to previously?

Practice observing. Set a timer for 10 minutes and just write about the world around you. All you're doing is reporting: "A squirrel just ran across a limb of the white oak . . ." and "This is boring. Why do I have to write for 10 minutes?" Let your thoughts freely associate.

Timed writing will help loosen the bindings on your subconscious. Repeated use of this exercise will unearth all sorts of interesting tidbits you've been storing away from your conscious mind. The subconscious is a treasure trove of intuitive knowings, and this exercise will help you gain insider access.

Studying the world around you will teach you about yourself . . . and understanding yourself will help you understand the world around you. Willow trees bend in the wind: you have the option to bend to the winds of change as well. Clear quartz stores information: you too can stow knowledge for future use. You are mirrored, and you are a mirror.

How are you a mirror to the natural world? How does the natural world reflect you?

When you look at another person and they feel unfathomable, look for emotions you are familiar with, like love or frustration or jealousy. What do you see of yourself in that other person? Does it change how you feel about them?

Everything you study or learn is filtered through the telescope of your perception, which is made up of thoughts, feelings, beliefs, smells, sounds, tastes, prejudices, blind spots, and . . . *stories.* Oh so many stories that you tell yourself about your worth, your lineage, your culture, your smarts. . . . You're made up of stories, stacked one atop the other, creating a psychological city only you can map.

The next time a strong thought, sensation, or emotion crosses your mind, ask yourself: *Really? Why?* Is there a story (or stories!) behind why you feel the way you feel?

In the midst of your studying and reflecting, don't forget to pause for self-care! Sometimes we forget what nurtures us, or our ideas get skewed by other people's ideas.

Think about what self-care truly means to you. What would feel divine right now? (And what's keeping you from doing it?)

Now let's look at what is influencing your perceptions. From social media to television to the friend who texts every afternoon, we are surrounded by other people's thoughts and feelings. Who's influencing you and what is the nature of their influence? Make a list. Remember, this is not just family and friends; this is also people on social media, the news outlets you turn to for information, the books you choose to read.

_____

_____

_____

_____

_____

_____

_____

_____

_____

_____

_____

_____

_____

_____

_____

_____

_____

_____

_____

_____

EXTRA CREDIT: After looking at this list, highlight the influencers that support your well-being, happiness, and mystical evolution. If you have friends who pull you down or you are listening to folks who make you feel small, think about shifting your social network.

How have the people in your life responded when you shared mystical experiences? How were you encouraged or discouraged from engaging with the world in this way? How did these experiences alter how you experienced magic for yourself?

Contemplate the ways in which your early perceptions of the mystic were altered or somehow made "normal." Or, if you are one of the lucky ones who were encouraged to grow into the world of magic and mystery, reflect on how your perceptions have grown and changed and what paths you took to achieve this growth. What did you think about magic when you were young? How has imagination factored into your life? Have you ever had trancelike experiences or instances of "seeing" things: ghosts, invisible friends, fairies? Have you explored things like astrology or tarot?

Identify places where you are overly rational or skeptical, where you discourage your own mystical thinking.

Write about your earliest memory of something that felt magical. Did you hear voices? Have an invisible friend or talk to the family cat? Did you know who was coming to visit before they showed up?

*I*s it in the blood? What does DNA mean for your mystical life? What is the place of blood and of blood ancestors in your magical work? There is no one answer to this question, but exploring it will give you insight into who you are and who you want to become.

How closely should DNA be tied to our individual search for a path to the mystery and magic of life? How do you feel about learning from, and in turn, sharing with, those who are from cultures that are outside your most recent blood-bound heritage? Do you feel it's necessary to create rules for yourself or others around the cross-cultural sharing of mystical experiences? Why or why not?

Lineage is not just genetics and family connections: it's the acknowledgment of the energies that support you. Who and what has supported you as you have grown into yourself?

If you are at odds with your family of origin or out-of-sync with the religious codes you grew up with, acknowledging a lineage of learning can help you feel a part of something that stretches back through the ages. Lineage anchors you to ancestral energy—whether those who came before share your DNA, your passion for botany, or your love of the stars.

Anchor your spiritual identity by drawing the family tree of your mystical lineage. Include those who are blood relations (if you so choose), as well as relations in your intellectual lineage, a lineage of craft, or a lineage of affiliation, as a way of anchoring your spiritual identity.

*L*et's dive into divination! There are patterns swirling all around you, and recognizing a pattern when you see it is a skill necessary for divining. Practice this heightened awareness not only during the Night but also throughout the day. Make it your new normal to pay attention to the sighs of the wind, the flight paths of the birds, the ways people stand on the subway, and the whispers of the leaves . . . they all have a story to tell if you're willing to listen. What patterns have you recently noticed?

*L*ook for shifts and changes to the usual patterns you've come to see. If, for example, you spot three wild turkeys over the course of a week and you usually see none, pay closer attention. What are the wild turkeys doing? Do a little research: do wild turkeys migrate? Open yourself up to changes that might be happening in the physical world or in the unseen realms of spirit. What breaks in the pattern are drawing your attention?

Sketching can get your brain to shift gears from judging and meaning-making into simply noticing.

Draw either the room you are sitting in or an object within that space. It's this act of close observation, which occurs when you put pen or pencil to paper, that matters, not the final drawing. Pay attention to details and edges, and how objects relate to each other. Ferreting out this level of detail will help you decipher the nuances of your visions, dreams, and divinations.

Divinations are signposts on your trail. They can offer you peace and a moment of connection, or they can jar you into reassessing everything you thought you believed. The creative challenge is in deciding how to work with what you learn and uncovering how it will enrich your life.

A divination, no matter how it's done, exists in relation to a query. It's important to ask the right question.

Compare these two queries and note down the differences:
What should I do next?
versus
Should I take the new position I was offered today?

___

Now compare these two:
Should I take the new position I was offered today?
versus
Will I be happy in the new position I was offered today?

Write about your experience with divination thus far. What tools have you used? Pendulums, smoke, freewriting, dreaming, scrying, pattern work, tarot cards, astrology, and tea leaves are some examples. How did they work for you? What were the results? If you've never divined before, what tools interest you? What activates your intuition?

To craft a query, start by writing down the first question that comes to your mind. Don't overthink it.

Now edit that question to make it more specific.

Ask yourself now if your edited question is detailed enough. Think about what you really want to know, what you're actually seeking.

CLEAR YOUR MIND BEFORE YOU DIVINE!

A *tabula rasa* was the ancient Roman equivalent of a blank notepad. Instead of being made of paper, it was made with wax. The wax was "blanked" by heating it and then smoothing it out. The same tablet could then be used over and over. A tabula rasa is like a new moon evening when the stars are obscured: an inky void, full of nothing but possibility.

Before you begin a divination, you'll want to blank your mind. By creating this tabula rasa, you're preparing yourself both mentally and energetically to receive clearly.

There are a few ways to do this:

* Breathe deeply, pulling clarity and quiet in through your lungs, exhaling everything that doesn't belong to you and your energy body.

* Soak in a tub of salt water, "salting out" energies that aren't yours so you can send them down the drain.

* Burn incense, letting the smoke waft through your aura and allowing the cleansing properties of the herbs to get into your metaphysical nooks and crannies while the scent soothes your nerves and quiets your mind.

* Grab a rattle or make one, and shake, letting the vibration dislodge even the most stubborn metaphysical muck.

How does it feel to have a blank mind? Do you feel ready to receive new information?

Let's focus on interpreting symbols and divinations. Choose a symbol that you're fond of—for example, a raven or spiral. Research this symbol's meaning across multiple cultures. Notice whether your chosen symbol appears in a multiplicity of cultural myths, folklores, designs, and sacred rites. Compare how the symbol is used across cultures.

$\mathcal{N}$ow think about why you chose this symbol. Can you see the collective unconscious running through your own thoughts?

The subconscious is a private and personal space, while the collective unconscious is a place where the threads of the world converge. It's also where we, collectively, store the symbols and myths that fuel our imagination, dreams, and divinations.

We use the collective unconscious when interpreting divinations, but the collective unconscious alone isn't enough when it comes to uncovering the meaning. Solid interpretation skills come not just from understanding universal symbolism, but from pairing universal symbolism with knowledge of how you yourself think—because *you* are the lens through which the divination or dream is being viewed.

Work on interpreting the symbolism of these four things, beginning with history and mythology, then looking at modern scientific and/or engineering information, moving on to take a gander at known symbolism, and ending with your personal reflection on how these symbols resonate through the lens of *you*.

* An owl
* A diamond
* A rowan tree
* A circular staircase

Craft a short essay that contemplates the effect of the collective unconscious in our global intellectual history *OR* ponder the role of Night thoughts on our daytime discoveries.

Divination is, at its heart, a form of intuitive knowing. *Do you trust your own intuition and intuitive ways of knowing?* Reflect for a few moments, perhaps as you sip your dream-time tea, on what you accept as truth and what you expect from different kinds of truth. *If a friend tells you she saw something in a dream, what weight do you give her revelations? If you consult your tarot deck for advice on a particular situation, what weight do you give the reading?*

*L*et's divine through freewriting. Write your question at the top of the page, then set a timer for 10 minutes or put on some music so you can use the length of a song to keep time (a song is usually about 3–4 minutes long). Take a few deep breaths of the Night air and let your eyes go soft. Then start writing! The goal is to keep your pen moving across the page, even if you feel like you're writing nonsense. At a certain point, your ego will step aside, and that is when the magic happens!

Writing is a fabulous tool for connection. If you want to connect with a plant, animal, crystal, or even one of your ancestors, ask it/them/him/her to share, then let your hand flow across the page. Don't worry about making sense of your writing: write first, interpret later.

Oneiromancy is a fancy word for using dreams as a method of divination. Here's your deceptively simple setup for dream divination:

* Place this journal and a pen on your nightstand within easy reach.

* Before going to sleep, sit on the edge of your bed. Take a few deep breaths with your feet flat on the floor. Set your question in your mind, with the intention that you will dream on it and remember your dream.

* When you wake up, stay very still so you don't scare your dream away.

* Replay what you remember of your dream while your eyes are still closed, moving the dream from image to words in your mind.

* When you feel like you've caught it, reach for your journal. Try to keep your movements minimal. Don't even turn on the light.

* Begin writing. List big ideas and images first so you don't lose them, then go back and write the dream as a story. Use the first-person present tense *(I am walking through a moonlit garden* instead of *she walked through a moonlit garden).*

The final step is interpretation. How do you interpret what happened in your dream?

_____

_____

_____

_____

_____

_____

_____

If you're having trouble remembering your dreams, mugwort is a traditional aid. The tea isn't tasty, but try a few sips before bed or burn some mugwort incense before you fall asleep.

Awaking dream is an act of purposeful imagining. You may feel like you're making up the images you're seeing, but that's *exactly* what you need to do to get a waking dream going.

Write your question at the top of the page, then choose some soothing music and light a few candles. Set a timer for 20 minutes. Allow your mind to relax and go soft. Let your shoulders ease and your facial muscles rest. Let your inner vision take over.

What did you see? How do you interpret what you saw?

Divine using a reflective surface, like a mirror, water, or polished brass or stone. These surfaces are often used for *scrying:* reading messages and guidance through reflection.

Write your question at the top of the page, then choose your reflective surface. Quiet your mind with a few full breaths. Hold your question in your mind as you gaze into the reflection. Keep your eyes relaxed. Let your mind flow. Note what you see using the present tense. (Don't overthink it!) How do you interpret what you saw?

Read the leaves . . . or the bones . . . or the stones! As usual, begin with a well-crafted question.

Bones, sticks, and stones are usually shaken and thrown. With tea leaves and coffee grounds, the tea or coffee is consumed, and the leaves or grounds left at the bottom of the cup are read. Over the long history of divination, people have read everything from oil to flour to ink stains, so don't feel limited to the exact things mentioned here: ask your question and scatter rice, beans, or spaghetti sticks from your kitchen!

After throwing down, soften your gaze and look for patterns.

Interpreting these patterns is very similar to how you work with tarot or oracle cards. Before you pull out a book of symbolism, first notice your intuitive hits . . . observe and note down what you see, think, and feel. Remember, you're using your Night-brain, allowing things to flow and connect— even if your day-brain is having a conniption fit about wasting perfectly good beans!

Our daytime brains now know that the four elements—Earth, Air, Water, and Fire—are not the primary building blocks of the universe. Instead we have atoms as their component parts. And yet our Night-brains hardly seem to notice this newish knowledge: our romance with the four elements remains.

Keep track of your relationship with the four elements. What schools of thought have influenced how you perceive them? Which elements appear in your Night-life and in what form? Are you dreaming of fire or water? Meditating with crystals (earth) or incense (air)?

Do a little world tour by research and catalog how many cultures around the globe have a concept similar to the idea of the four elements. See if you can date the origin of these thought patterns in various cultures. How many cultures were involved in an almost simultaneous discovery of similar elemental principles?

What do you think of the idea of including a fifth element—ether, space, or the void—into the League of Elements? What would the properties of this fifth element be?

Alchemy is concerned with change and transformation. How might you go about using the alchemy of the four elements—either metaphorically or materially—to create a change in your own life?

Your thought process might look something like this:

I've been so angry at (insert the name of the person whom you're holding a grudge against) for a long time. When I think of this person, my heart feels like a stone. Stone is Earth. Things grow in Earth and plantings break up compacted soil allowing Air and Water to come through. Maybe I can imagine planting a rosebush in the hurt place in my heart and tending to it every day. Perhaps this would let my emotions (Water) flow and allow new thoughts (Air) to influence my feelings.

This exercise might sound absolutely intimidating. Don't panic! This is a creative exercise, not a quiz. So put on your Night-goggles, relax, and contemplate the wind blowing your intimidation away.

Explore your personal elemental makeup! Choose one of these systems to experiment with: Ayurveda or Wu Xing. For both, you can find online quizzes to determine your constitutional type. (The English-language search term for Wu Xing is "five element" so look up "five elements quiz.") While these quizzes aren't perfect, you'll learn all sorts of things about yourself, including the best foods to eat for your constitution and, depending on the quiz, which colors to wear to boost your elemental balance.

*L*et's explore a different kind of Night sky than most of us experience:

Start with a swirl of stars—the brightest look like sharp pinpricks, while the lightest blur together to form a fabric of shimmering light. The sky itself feels like it's curving overhead in an almost-visible dome above you. Tonight is the Night of the dark moon: there are no other lights in the sky beyond the stars themselves. The modern world falls away. Maybe it's 2,000 years ago . . . maybe two million. It's just you, the Earth at your back, and the stars above.

If you had no knowledge of Nicolaus Copernicus's heliocentric theory—that's the one that put the sun at the center of our universe—or the astronauts of Apollo 11 doing a moon walk, what story might you tell about the stars and their relationship to the Earth and to you?

Choose three ancient cultures from different parts of the globe and read a few of their earliest tales. (Need ideas? Try Babylonian, Maori, and Tibetan or Phoenician, Aztec, and Mongolian.) Pay attention to where the people live and where the gods reside. How did these stories impact the ways in which people thought about the Night sky when they were standing under it looking up?

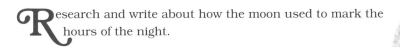

Research and write about how the moon used to mark the hours of the night.

One of the oldest forms of divination is astrology—you can't understand the Night without it! Do some research on your astrological Sun sign—the sign tied to the month of your birth. Are there stories associated with it? Does it have a ruling god or goddess?

Grab a compass, a star map, and a flashlight, then walk outside (if you're day-reading, do this tonight). Use your compass to orient yourself. Before you look up, set a question in your heart, the same way you did in your divination practice. Keep it simple like: *What message do you have for me tonight? Or what do I need to know about the coming weeks?* Then . . . look up. What catches your eye first? Hint: if it's moving, it's a planet, meteor, satellite, airplane, or space invaders. If this moving object is the primary focus for you, look to see which stars form the wallpaper behind it. Based on the direction you're facing, you can use your star map to figure out which constellation is waving to you. If you are drawn to a single star, see which constellation it's a part of.

After you have the constellation figured out, head indoors and research its stories. Think about how what you're learning is applicable to the question you asked. Interpret the star stories in the same way you would read a tarot or oracle card.

_____

_____

_____

_____

_____

_____

_____

_____

_____

_____

A couple things to layer into your reading:

* If it was a moving object that called your attention to a particular region of the heavens, add the idea of motion and movement into the stewpot of your interpretation.

* If it was a single star that lit your eye, look at where that star sits in the larger constellation. What layers does this add to your thoughts?

* You could look to the east and see what constellation is rising, asking the question what is rising in my own life?

* Or you could look west and see what is setting, asking the question what is setting in my own life?

* Or you could look at the shapes formed by the stars, put on your Night-goggles, allow your eyes to go soft, and write your own story.

Craft a piece of your own mythology. Take one event or period of your life, pull out your compass, put on your Night-goggles, and rewrite it as a Hero's Journey. Find the patterns at work in your own life and reframe hardships into learning experiences. The Hero's Journey is all about the alchemy of personal transformation.

Identify the *Hero's Journey* in the Wild

Watch a movie of your choice and map the Hero's Journey through the story line. Start with epic adventures like *Star Wars, The Princess Bride, The Hunger Games, Spider-Man,* or any movie that played on a main stage.

After you have identified the patterns within your Hero's Journey, go back and see if they align with movements in your personal astrology chart or, if your story takes place over a shorter period of time, with the phases of the moon.

Use your divination skills to interpret your Hero's Journey and foresee what's next.

Brainstorm at least 10 ways you can create a direct relationship for yourself with the Night sky. What practices can you put in place to enhance your Night vision and allow Night ways of being to balance your daytime self?

There are no answers,
only questions enough
to fill the Night sky.